DOCTORING IN NICARAGUA

poems by

Greg Stidham

Finishing Line Press
Georgetown, Kentucky

DOCTORING IN NICARAGUA

Copyright © 2021 by Greg Stidham
ISBN 978-1-64662-482-9 First Edition
All rights reserved under International and Pan-American Copyright Conventions. No part of this book may be reproduced in any manner whatsoever without written permission from the publisher, except in the case of brief quotations embodied in critical articles and reviews.

ACKNOWLEDGMENTS

I wish to thank the editors of the following publications who published these poems in their current or an earlier form:

"Holding a Baby" and "Osteosarcoma" ~ *Blood and Thunder: Musings on the Art of Medicine*, Autumn, 2019
"New Epileptic," "Doctoring in Nicaragua," and "The Lock," ~ *Intima: A Journal of Narrative Medicine*
"Tetralogy of Fallot," *Examined Life Journal*, Fall/Winter, 2018

I also wish to acknowledge and thank Peter Sims, Harley Gallagher, and my wife, Pam, all of whom provided crucial feedback during the process of preparing this chapbook.

Publisher: Leah Huete de Maines
Editor: Christen Kincaid
Cover Art: M.P. Tully
Author Photo: Pam K. Stidham
Cover Design: Elizabeth Maines McCleavy

Order online: www.finishinglinepress.com
also available on amazon.com

Author inquiries and mail orders:
Finishing Line Press
PO Box 1626
Georgetown, Kentucky 40324
USA

Table of Contents

Introduction

Ode to a Medical Resident 1

Claire 2

Holding a Baby 3

The Lock 4

Osteosarcoma 5

Alive 6

Tell it Slant 7

Doctoring in Nicaragua 8

Lucy 9

Central Market, Managua 10

El Niño Patiente 11

Tetralogy of Fallot 12

Imagine 13

Lament for the Parents 14

Parent Support Group 15

She talks with her dead daughter, ... 16

Bereavement 17

New Epileptic 18

Anatomy Lab 19

Recovery from Total Knee Replacement 20

Colonoscopy 21

Doctor Bag 22

Old People 23

Introduction

I retired from medicine in 2012 after a 35-year career as a pediatric ICU physician. I had trained in Pediatric Critical Care Medicine in preparation for caring for the most critically ill and injured children. With such a high-risk population of patients, positive outcomes were not always guaranteed, and I learned on the job about caring for parents and families during their most terrible times. These children and their parents have become emblazoned on my soul.

During my years in medicine, I repressed another self—the self that wanted to embrace creative writing, especially poetry. I never abandoned that self, and wrote, though sporadically, throughout my medical career. After retiring, however, I was at last able to plunge headlong and seriously into the vocation of creative writing.

Since that transition, I have written in several genres, with satisfaction and some success. But poetry has been my greatest passion. Not surprisingly, some of the poetry I have written is informed by my experiences over the years in medicine. This collection is an acknowledgment of the influence my medical experiences have had on my poetry.

The collection can be viewed as having four influences: my experiences in patient care; experiences with loss and bereavement, and trying to be helpful to grieving parents; my work on a new pediatric cardiac surgery program in Nicaragua; and my personal experiences with my own medical frailties.

I offer these not as a poetic memoir. Rather, I share these poems because of my belief that they speak to some greater truth than merely my personal experiences which gave them birth. I hope that some of the poems will resonate with readers and that they will reach beyond the words of the poems themselves.

Ode to a Medical Resident Who Writes Poetry
  after Adam Possner

Taking the train
Columbia to Baltimore
an hour plus,
clattering noise
travelers' noses
buried deep in the Sun,
no talk, a few
take-out coffees
still sipped.
So, I embrace these fellow
sleepy travelers, take up my pen
and begin to sketch
the notes of a poem.

Claire

Enamored of my magic tricks—
cheap plastic props—she'd still smile
(perhaps just humoring me)
who'd made her pale face
turn beet red when I asked her
to be my girlfriend. Ten years old
and nearly hairless, like me,
but she tried to hide it
with blue bandanas
and ponytail elastic bands
for the few remaining
coarse strands.
I had a bad
feeling about her, a feeling
neither medical nor definable,
a feeling before I even knew
she'd asked her nurse
if she were going to die.
And we pumped on her chest,
and we injected her
with heart-reviving drugs,
but her heart just kept quitting until
finally, I said "Stop. Enough."

I dreamed of her later.

My colleague saw my grief
and gave me a scapular-like cloth icon
of the sort that I knew from my childhood,
but which doesn't exist in his faith,
and he told me to wear it for 30 days.

Holding a Baby

Sometimes things seem
so simple, so certain,
like the still-warm body
of the infant girl
born with the fallible heart
held by her young aunt
when her parents couldn't.
When the aunt asked
"would you like to hold her?"
--so simple, so certain,
so obvious a choice:
take that body, hold it
like a living infant,
my own perhaps,
and not like the child
whose heart I couldn't
coax to continue.

The Lock

In the dim room with curtained glass walls,
monitors dark and quiet, I watched him.
With tiny manicure scissors,
the type used to trim a baby's nails,
he snipped a strand of hair
from the very back of the boy's still head—
a near-perfect blond ringlet
he gently slid into a zip-lock baggie.
Pausing, he placed the lock
in the outer pocket of his duffle bag,
likely stuffed with clean and dirty socks,
and underwear from three bedside days
and endless nights sleeping stiffly
in an overstuffed chair.
He kissed the boy's forehead,
stood, and turned,
nodding to me
and walked out the door.

Osteosarcoma

Eight-year old amputee
attempting wheelchair wheelies,
caroms off hallway litters and
stops, points to the bandaged
thigh-stump, "Wanna see me
wiggle my *little* leg?"

Alive

The young doctor at dusk
in the darkened room of the ICU
held the baby's body,
and he cried and cried,
and knew that he was alive.

Tell it slant

Sometimes I find
telling it slant is hard.
The pain supersedes restraint
and clever convention,
even imaginative metaphor.
I cannot help myself
and I write it straight on,
not slant, and birth a poem
that fails to resonate.

Doctoring in Nicaragua

Like an old-time silent movie
my memories of Managua flicker
in faded black and white
halting and jerking, just
like the tiny taxis darting
round the roundabouts
punctuating the city's boulevards.

Nurses in starchy white uniforms,
housekeepers with mops at attention,
black-haired children with zippered chests,
healing hearts beating beneath bandages
with the newfound certainty of a metronome.

Lucy

>*for Lucy Cantillano Reyes,*
>*9/29/89-1/15/06*

Lucy in the sky,
with or without diamonds,
Lucy's in the sky, her
broken heart soaring, split
and stapled sternum not
hurting any more, and you
watching your mother, watching
out for your mother as she
makes her way to your Nicaraguan
mountain home, are you
glad that it is over? are you
mad that we fought
as hard as we did, refused
to let you go?
I don't think so, it
wouldn't seem the you
I got to know through
the sleights of my imagination,
Lucy, in the sky.

Central Market, Managua

Squalor on three sides.
Ahead, booths aplenty
filled with geriatric fruits,
others with rancid meats
hanging from splintered rafters,
chickens and pigs,
poor people hawking goods:
toothpaste and fake leather belts,
hammocks and wood carvings,
but then the women
beating dough with bare fists
making tortillas on hot
skillet surfaces, all in rhythm,
like hearing prayers
while attending Mass.

El Niño Patiente
Managua, Nicaragua. 2004

hospital infantile
treetop fall and
fractured liver
big vein ripped
clean   you
were supposed to
die

el niño now drills
doctors and nurses
straight shooter squirt gun
catches rubber balls with
hands like a genteel
pianist's, fingers
long and slender,
arms hardly fuller

Tetralogy of Fallot

Fingers like drumsticks,
clubbed ends capable of
fast triplets and rim shots
like the masters—
Philly Joe Jones and Art Blakey,
Billy Higgins, Roy Haynes—
while the irregular heart
strikes the syncopated
backbeat of the bass lines,
borrows from the undercurrent
of the blues: blue lips,
blue fingertips.

Imagine
>*for the many children
I could not save*

Imagine the unimaginable.
Imagine Neil Armstrong leaping
thirty feet above lunar dust,
proclaiming the first small step for man.

Imagine 40 days of torrential monsoon
observed from the deck of a wooden ship
packed tight with pairs of wild animals,
imagine

the pounding on the door in 1939, the
thunder of bootfall in the black night,
your night-dressed father hustled away.

Imagine your father and your mother
digging their graves at Choeung Ek,

or you, running before your
napalm-slathered burning sister,
imagine.

But imagine fishing
the limp blue body
of your two-year old
only son from the swimming pool
of your best friend, lifeless.

Or holding your newborn infant,
congenital heart disease, at the end,
watching the ventilator turned off,
and hearing the monitor beeps
slow to silence.

Imagine
       imagine.

Lament for the Parents

This pain is like no other
that I've never felt,
except through small pieces
shared by those who have,
parents who've lost a child—
hearts broken at birth,
fishing trip accidents,
bacteria in the blood,
wide-eyed encounters with
drunken drivers.

Hundreds of parents have shared
a piece of that unimaginable pain with me.
I've watched a mother hold her infant
wrapped in dishtowel-sized
blue-trimmed baby blankets,
while lips paled almost indiscernibly.
I've turned off breathing machines,
removed from windpipes breathing tubes,
turned off beeping monitors so
the slowing blip of the bouncing light
would not distract.
I've helped bathe their bodies
before placing them
in the outstretched arms
of their parents.

Parent Support Group
Villanelle for a Dead Child

In a circle they sat, warriors in a wigwam,
tears hidden by lenses and Kleenex
as they told their stories one by one.

Teen sons cliff-jumping into cold waters,
backseat home-bound sons with dad after hockey,
in a circle they sat, warriors in a wigwam.

A mute girl, wheelchair-bound eight years,
left her father to tell her story to ten strangers,
as they told their stories one by one.

The divorcée decided to become a mother—
fertility clinics, anonymous donor,
in a circle they sat, warriors in a wigwam.

Two twins came three months early, living on machines,
riding a roller coaster's highs and lows, till one died.
They told their stories one by one,

swapping terrible tales, their children all dead.
Who can understand but the ones in the circle,
the circle where they sat, warriors in a wigwam?

Despair and deadly pain, they all felt it just the same.
They felt guilty and angry, sometimes suicidal.
In a circle they sat, warriors in a wigwam,
as they told their stories one by one.

She Talks with her Dead Daughter,
    after Jo McDougall

she mourns her words that fall apart,
or flail like a pitchfork thrashing hay
    wildly into empty air.
She, ordained alone to preserve her,
    feels guilt for forgetting for an eyeblink,
    and for her failing words.

I too talk to the dead, and
I too feel guilt,
    my words too vanish
    like breath on a winter day.

Bereavement

He mentioned it, the anniversary.
His sister, breast cancer, four years ago.
The talk was supposed to be
about his son and his wife,
their fiery accident a year ago.
Instead he remembered
her practical jokes,
and he wept.

New Epileptic

Stooping now
to retrieve a dropped pen
then standing again,
an act so ordinary
the brief passing
vertigo once
unnoticed now
triggers thoughts
of unruly neurons
plotting their next
choreography, the next
slapstick they'll direct
at my expense,
my pride,
perhaps even
my breath.

Anatomy Lab

Imagining them now
I can see them—
medical students in fifteen years,
four-strong, gathered scalpel-handed
around me about to see first-hand
my many foibles.

I wonder what they'll think
of the adipose apron
I swore I'd never have.

Which will discover delighted
the detached half biceps
that made me flexing
look like Popeye the Sailorman,
after spinach?

Maybe they will find the reason
my shoulder is so sore it
wakes me at night and makes me
a right-sided-only sleeper.

And the MS plaques I have seen on MRI,
they will see first-hand, denied
even to me up-close-and-personal
they'll touch and slide their fingers
along the slickness and

will they wonder if these glistening
white sheets made me think differently,
or less well, or love less,
or dream better, I wonder,
will they wonder anything at all?

Recovery from Total Knee Replacement

I try hard to be stoic, not complain
about the knee pain trying to stand,
and the quick lightning up my leg
with every step.

Then there is the foot swelling
so grand my feet look like softballs,
or heads of a caveman's clubs,
the skin so tight you can't
indenture it anymore—it doesn't "pit,"
but feels like it could burst
open at any moment,
like a water balloon,
the skin starting to blister.

I am tired of the wearying walk to
the toilet, where I balance myself
between two narrow walls trying
to keep my aim true.

And God I am so tired
of injecting my belly roll each
morning with heparin to help
ensure that clots don't form in my legs.

Most of all the exercises,
stretching, strengthening, all after icing,
are like pre-Olympic training,
and leave me feeling
so ever muscle sore,
but also better.

Give it three to four months, they say.
I can wait. I guess.

Colonoscopy

knives stabbing
from the inside
tried holding still
tried spartan brave
but privately craved
versed   anything
then there it was
on the tv screen
short-stalked mushroom
red   juicy red
looking back at me
my own private polyp

Doctor Bag

On graduation day they all came,
parents, grandmother, and new wife.
My white-haired grandmother
gave me a card, with a small check.
And my classmates spilled beer
provided on the patio, where
my parents handed me their gift—
a large, black leather and burnished
brass buckled "doctor bag."
These bags don't exist now,
or even then, except for Norman Rockwell.
I didn't know what I could do
with such a fine handbag,
and it has sat on shelves
in home offices in many cities
while I contemplated dying children.
And I remembered my parents
and the leather bag,
but I don't remember
my wife even being there.

Old People

We live out our lives
like two old people,
and I can't understand how
till I realize we are
two old people.
We sit on the patio
on the side of our house
enjoying the first days
of long overdue spring,
but still too imperfect
to sit without sweaters
and a propane gas heater,
watching the sun setting
behind the leafless but budding
maples and black ashes,
while walkers pass
our corner tree,
the "humor tree,"
plastered with New Yorker cartoons
and the "Poem of the Week,"
pausing sometimes
to glance and laugh,
more rarely to read.

Greg Stidham is a pediatric intensivist (ICU physician) who retired in 2012 after a 32-year career in academic medicine. In retirement he has been able to resurrect his passion for literature and creative writing. He has published a memoir, numerous pieces of short fiction and creative non-fiction, but his real passion has been and is poetry.

After 28 years at the children's hospital in Memphis, and the University of Tennessee, he moved to Kingston, Ontario, where he assumed a similar position at Queen's University and Kingston Health Sciences Center. He currently serves as a volunteer grief counselor for bereaved parents through Bereaved Families of Ontario. He continues to live and write in Kingston with his wife, Pam, and Dexter, the last survivor of their ever-evolving pack of rescue dogs.

www.ingramcontent.com/pod-product-compliance
Lightning Source LLC
LaVergne TN
LVHW041519070426
835507LV00012B/1677